Little Red Book
of
Phonics

By the same author

CATEGORY I

Language skills for all age groups from Class 1 onwards: Little Red Book Series

CATEGORY II

For beginners: A Child's First Dictionary (Little Red Book Series)

CATEGORY III

To develop a love for reading among schoolchildren and also for adults, a collection of the best stories by renowned writers: Masterpieces of World Fiction series, *50 Greatest Short Stories*.

CATEGORY IV

For developing quiz instinct and general awareness: The Fun Fact series—*Fun with Numbers, Fun with Riddles*, etc.; *A2Z Quiz Book; The Book of Firsts and Lasts; The Things You Ought to Know* series—*National Surroundings and Game Time, 100 Events that Changed the World, Amazing India Facts*

CATEGORY V

Motivational books: *The Book of Virtues, The Book of Motivation*

CATEGORY VI

For overall preparation and general awareness: *The Students' Companion*

CATEGORY VII

Teachers' reference book: *A2Z Book of Word Origins, The Ultimate Book of Common Errors, Treasure Chest of Public Speaking*

Little Red Book *of* Phonics

Terry O'Brien

Published by
Rupa Publications India Pvt. Ltd 2018
7/16, Ansari Road, Daryaganj
New Delhi 110 002

Sales centres:
Allahabad Bengaluru Chennai
Hyderabad Jaipur Kathmandu
Kolkata Mumbai

Copyright © Terry O'Brien 2018

The views and opinions expressed in this book are the author's own and the facts are as reported by him which have been verified to the extent possible, and the publishers are not in any way liable for the same.

All rights reserved.
No part of this publication may be reproduced, transmitted, or stored in a retrieval system, in any form or by any means, electronic, mechanical, photocopying, recording or otherwise, without the prior permission of the publisher.

ISBN: 978-93-5304-013-0

First impression 2018

10 9 8 7 6 5 4 3 2 1

Printed by Excel Printers Pvt. Ltd., New Delhi

Typeset by Chetan Sharma

This book is sold subject to the condition that it shall not, by way of trade or otherwise, be lent, resold, hired out, or otherwise circulated, without the publisher's prior consent, in any form of binding or cover other than that in which it is published.

*'Children are made readers
on the laps
of their parents.'*

—Emilie Buchwald

Introduction

Phonics is a literacy method that is as old as the alphabet itself. Ever since people learned to read and write, they learnt the letters and the sounds they made. This was almost 3,200 years old. However, in the twentieth century the *whole language* method was seen as an alternative. This theory was based on the system that children learnt the local language without formal training.

One should not get confused with the two terms: PHONICS and PHONETICS. Phonics is a method to teach people to read and write; phonetics is the science of speech sounds. Phonetics has its own alphabet. It has technical terms, and it is not directly concerned with teaching literary skills.

Explicit systematic phonics instruction is the most effective way to teach children how to read. Without it, some children will end up having serious reading difficulties.

Phonics helps your child learn to read and spell. Without this ability, your child cannot be fully literate. Words are like codes, and phonics teaches children how to crack the reading code. Phonics is, therefore, an important part of any reading development programme.

Phonics: teaching children the sounds made by individual letter or letter groups (for example, the letter 'c' makes a *k* sound), and teaching children how to merge separate sounds together to make it one word (for example, blending the sounds *k, a, t* makes CAT). This type of phonics teaching is often referred to as 'synthetic phonics'.

Explicit: directly teaching children the specific

associations between letters and sounds, rather than expecting them to gain this knowledge indirectly.

Systematic: English has a complicated spelling system. It is important to teach letter sound mappings in a systematic way, beginning with simple letter sound rules and then moving onto more complex associations.

It is often best to start learning to read through phonics from preschool to 2nd grade or from about ages 3 to 8. This book also has a pronunciation and intonation unit for teacher-taught purposes.

Although one learns to speak not each one learns to read and write.

Literacy must be taught.

Happy learning

Terry O'Brien

Contents

Introduction ... 9

1. Phonics ... 11

2. Pronunciation ... 37

3. Intonation ... 91

PHONICS

RUDIMENTS OF PHONICS

'Phonics' comes from the Greek word *phone* meaning 'voice' or 'sound'. It is a method of learning to read and write English that concentrates on sounds; it deals with the sounds the letters make. It is a method that uses the alphabet as its base.

In contrast to this is 'Whole Language' method which ignores the sounds of the letters. It makes us look at each word in the English language as a whole unit. Whole Language methods do deal with the sounds the individual letters make.

The Alphabet

The alphabet is actually a sound code; each letter stands for a particular sound.

SOUNDS of the LETTERS

Basic letter sounds

a: apple

b: bird

c: cat

d: dog

e: egg

f: frog

g: goat

h: house

i: insect
j: jug
k: kite
l: log
m: moon
n: nest
o: orange
p: pig
q: queen
r: robot
s: sun
t: tap
u: umbrella
v: violin
w: whale
x: box
y: yoyo
z: zebra

Note: These letter sounds are not to be confused with the name of each letter. We usually recite the letter names when we spell a word. We say See, Ay, Tee when the word spells cat. The word cat is made up of three sounds —c! a! and t! If you run these sounds together, you get the word cat.

Note: The pronunciations of words are formed by letter sounds put together, not letter names put together!

THE NAME OF THE LETTERS

a	ay	n	En
b	Bee	o	Oh
c	See	p	Pea
d	Dee	q	Queue
e	Ee	r	Are
f	Eff	s	Ess
g	Jee	t	Tee
h	Aitch or Haitch	u	You
i	Eye	v	Vee
j	Jay	w	Double-you
k	Kay	x	Ex
l	Ell	y	Why
m	Em	z	Zed or Zee

The Beginning Point

The phonic approach begins by teaching students to recognize the letters of the alphabet and the sounds they make. As soon as this is accomplished, it is already possible to read many English words. All we need to do is "decode" them. We see the word cat on the page, for instance, and we convert the letters into sounds—c! a! t! We run these sounds together and we can read the word cat.

Phonics is Easier

The phonics helps us recognize the letters and the typical sounds they make. This in turn helps one decipher or read large words. Words like tunnel, trumpet, pond, picnic and confident—they can all be sounded out. If you know the basic sounds the letters make (for example, b: boy, z: zebra, etc.) you run them together.

— SOUNDING WORDS —

By learning the basic sounds of twenty-six symbols, we can already decipher hundreds of English words.

Digraphs

Phonics has more to it than just learning the *twenty-six*

letters of the alphabet and the basic sounds they make. Indeed, the English language has more sounds than there are letters to make them. There are about *forty-four speech sounds* and only twenty-six letters.

Note: TOO MANY SOUNDS: 44 into 26 won't go!

The solution to this problem is the use of digraphs, i.e. *two or more letters are sometimes used together to indicate a new sound*—a sound different from the basic sounds of the letters put together.

The letter-combinations **ch, tion, ous** and **or** are all **digraphs**. The digraph **ch** doesn't give you the sounds of c! + h! put together. It in fact gives you the new sound ch as in chalk.

Similarly, **tion** doesn't give you the sounds t+ i + n put together. No, it gives you tion as in nation. The same with all and or: The letters of these digraphs work together to produce a new sound. It is therefore by using letters together to form new sounds (mostly digraphs) that we are able to write all forty-four speech sounds with just twenty-six letters.

Spelling Made Easy

As soon as we start learning the English digraphs we can begin forming more complex words with ease. Take a word like *birthday*. It is composed of the basic letter sounds *b* and *d* and *three* digraphs, *ir*, *th* and *ay*. If we know these basic letter sounds and digraphs we will have no problem reading this word even if we have never come across it.

Note: A linguist can find more than 44 sounds in English.

Let's look at some other longer words and see how they break down into basic letter sounds and digraphs:

tea = t + ea

spoon = s + p + oo + n

freedom = f + r + ee + d + o + m

portion = p + or + tion

Extra Sounds

Sometimes letters don't make their basic sounds. They are often combined to create extra sounds. This is normal for digraphs. Sometimes even single letters are used to make a sound different from their basic sound. Two very common cases are the final e (as in *be*) and the final *y* (as in by) in very short words.

The Vowels

The **basic sounds** of the five common vowels a, e, i, o and u are often called short vowels.

Short Vowels:

a : apple

e : egg

i : insect

o : orange

u : for umbrella

The Basic Vowel Sounds:

Fat Cat	**a** as in **cat**
Big Pig	**i** as in **pig**
Bug Rug	**u** as in **bug**
Dot	**o** as in **dot**
Pet Hen	**e** as in **hen**
Fox Box	**o** as in **fox**
Run	**u** as in **bug**
Picnic	**i** as in **pig**

Single Letter Extra Sounds

In some English words, the longer vowel is represented by the single letter. For example, i : feet

Spelling Rules

To help children learn to read and write more accurately, we can also teach them certain spelling rules, i.e. rules along with the basic sounds, the digraphs and other extra sounds.

Phonics is a method for teaching reading and writing of the English language by developing learners' phonemic awareness—the ability to hear, identify and manipulate phonemes—in order to teach the correspondence between these sounds and the spelling patterns (graphemes) that represent them.

The goal of phonics is to enable beginning readers to decode new written words by sounding them out, or, in phonics terms, *blending* the sound-spelling patterns. This is a sub lexical approach and, as a result, is often contrasted with whole language, a word-level-up philosophy for teaching reading.

Rule 1:

An example of such a rule is what we must do when adding ing to a word that ends in a silent e. Here we are taught to drop the *e* when adding the ing (*bake*, for example, becomes *baking*, *give* becomes *giving*).

Rule 2:

Another rule concerns adding ing to a word with a short vowel (a basic vowel sound). Run, for instance, becomes *running* and *sit* becomes *sitting*. Here double the consonant to retain the short vowel sound.

Special Words

A special word is a word like *said*, which does not follow the rules of sounding out. The letters *ai* in the middle of *said* do not follow any rule. In such a case we have to learn the word by rote.

Two Sorts of Special Words:

1. Some special words, like said and any, are special and always will be special—we never learn rules that will enable us to sound them out. We call these very special words.

2. Other words, like *thorn*, are special only until we learn the rule(s) for them. When we learn the two digraphs *th* (as in *thin*) and or (as in *for*), the word thorn will cease to be special. It will be a regular, phonic word which we can sound out using the rules we know. This sort of word is a not-so-special word.

Some same-sounding digraphs:

ea as in heat	or	*ee* as in tree
aw as in paw	or	*or* as in sort
er as in fern	or	*ir* as in bird
ow as in how	or	*ou* as in loud
ew as in crew	or	*oo* as in roof

Indeed, phonic spelling principles are a huge aid to memory. The spelling of one word is remembered because it follows a rule, and the spelling of another is remembered because it does not follow the rule.

The Objectives of an Alphabet Book:

General Objective:

- To develop the English skills of listening, speaking, reading and writing.

- To teach students the basic sounds made by the letters of the alphabet.

Particular Objective:

To know the sound of the letter, to recognize the letter and to write the letter.

ACTIVITY

Using the listening ears game

- Teacher sounds out several words or non-words in separate sounds, e.g. words or non-words like b + a + t or s + ii + z.
- Teacher asks whether each set of letters is a real English word or not.

24 Consonant Phonemes/Graphemes

Phoneme (sound)	Examples		Graphemes (written patterns)
/b/	banana, bubbles	b	**bb**
/c/	car, duck	c	**k, ck, q, ch**
/d/	dinosaur, puddle	d	**dd,**
/f/	fish, giraffe	f	**ff, ph, gh**
/g/	guitar, goggles	g	**gg**
/h/	helicopter	h	
/j/	jellyfish, fridge	j	**g, dge, ge**

Little Red Book of Phonics

/l/	leaf, bell	l	**ll, le**
/m/	monkey, hammer	m	**mm, mb**
/n/	nail, knot	n	**nn, kn**
/p/	pumpkin, puppets	p	**pp**
/r/	rain, write	r	**rr, wr**
/s/	sun, mouse	s	**ss, ce, se, c, sc**
/t/	turtle, little	t	**tt**
/v/	volcano, halve	v	**ve**
/w/	watch, queen	w	**wh, u**
/x/	fox	x	
/y/	yo-yo	y	
/z/	zip, please	z	**zz, ze, s, se**

/sh/	shoes, television		**sh, ch, si, ti**
/ch/	children, stitch		**ch, tch**
/th/	mother		**th**
/th/	thong		**th**
/ng/	sing, ankle		**ng, n**

TIPS FOR TEACHERS AND PARENTS

Listen to the sounds around you

1. From a very young age children hear and respond to sounds in the environment. They quickly recognize familiar voices, respond to their name and express shock when they hear unfamiliar sounds (big bangs and sneezes, for example)—all part of living in and creating a sound-rich learning environment, which is the basis of phonics.

2. Make everyday sounds into learning tools by:

   Responding to sounds you hear. Make a big effort to include your child in the sounds around them too by asking them questions about what they can hear, for example: Can you hear the police car? What does it sound like? What noise is that dog making? What does the rain sound like?

3. Engage your child in lots of funny rhyming games and read lots of rhyming books, first pointing out the sounds to them and then encouraging them to create their own rhyming sounds.

Highlight initial sounds

Once your child is more attuned to hearing sounds in the environment, start drawing their attention to initial sounds at the beginning of words. Practical ways to do this include:

Stuttering out the initial sound of a word in order to drawing their attention to it: Please, can you pass the j j j jam? Please, can you get in the c c c car? You can play games with this, too, where they have to guess what you are going to say just by the initial sound, for example: 'Put your finger on your n n n... (pause to let them guess!) nose' or 'Would you like to eat a b b b... (banana)?'

Alliteration games

Find lots of alliteration opportunities (alliteration is when words start with the same sound), for example: She sells seashells on the shore/Daisy and Danny are dancing in the dark. It's also fun to think of alliteration names for all your friends and family (Marvellous Mummy/Delicious Daddy!).

Link letters and sounds

When shopping, encourage your child to look at the labels on food or to help you write the initial sound of a word on a shopping list: 'I need three things that start with a b (banana, bread and broccoli), so please, can you write me three bs on the list?'

Step-by-step blending

As your child's phonics learning progresses, you'll reach the 'blending' stage. It's time to hear all the sounds in the word and blend them together!

Teaching Phonics and Word Study

Phonics and word study are one of the five key areas of reading instruction; they are essential components that lay a solid foundation to read and spell successfully. There are four basic elements when teaching phonics and word study:

- Letter-sound knowledge
- Regular word reading
- Irregular word reading
- Decodable text reading

Letter-Sound Knowledge

Letter-sound knowledge refers to the understanding that letters and groups of letters in a word are associated with distinct sounds. Before reading a word, a child must blend the individual sounds of each letter together. Therefore, it is imperative that a child initially learns each letter's most common sound.

It is not recommended to teach letter sounds in alphabetic order but rather in clusters that can form numerous words. For example, the letters, /m/, /n/, /a/ and /t/ can be used to form several words, e.g. am, mat, tan. In addition, it is not recommended to initially introduce confusing letter-sound relationships. In particular, avoid teaching the following combinations simultaneously:

- /b/, /p/ and /d/

- /d/ and /q/

- /p/ and /q/

- /w/ and /m/

- /u/ and /n/

While every child's pace is slightly different, introducing two letter-sound relationships per week is ideal for most children.

Regular Word Reading

After a few weeks of letter-sound instruction, most children are ready for regular word reading. A child who knows the letter-sound association for /m/, /n/, /a/, /t/, /i/ and /s/ can decode words such as in, man, is and many more. The short /a/ sound should be one of the first taught—it is so common in the English language that learning this sound increases the words a child can read and write twofold. The next step requires a child to blend known sounds together to read a word. A child should silently sound out each sound and then say the whole word quickly.

It is recommended to begin teaching words with the following patterns:

- Short vowel–consonant (VC), e.g. it, in

- Consonant–short vowel–consonant (CVC), e.g. sit, tin

As a child progresses, introduce the more complex patterns:

- CCVC, e.g. shop, stop

- CVCC, e.g. last, list

- CCVCC, e.g. truck, trunk

- CVCe, e.g. bake, rake

As noted above, a child should begin with the consonant and short vowel sounds. Then introduce blends (two or more consonants that retain their own sound), digraphs (combining two letters to make one sound) and long vowel sounds.

Irregular Word Reading

According to Dr Moats, approximately 25 per cent of the most common words used in children's books are phonetically irregular. Irregular words and other very high frequency words are generally taught as whole words; these words are commonly referred to as sight words. It is recommended to teach irregular words that appear often in children's writings and texts; review these words prior to their encounter in a story. As you introduce new sight words, make sure you review the previously taught words. Finally, use these words in both reading and writing activities. For example, they can write two sight words ten times and then write a sentence using the words. Select books that contain the sight words you are currently reviewing.

Decodable Text Reading

After a child receives instruction in both regular and irregular words, they are ready to apply this knowledge and read a book. Try to select reading material that contains those letter-sound associations as well as sight words that a child has been taught. First, read the book together and then have the child reread the book.

Forty-four Most Frequent English Sounds

Sound	Keyword	Sound	Keyword
short /i/	It	/z/	zoom
/t/	Tip	/th/	that
/p/	Pig	/ch/	chill
/n/	Nose	/sh/	shop
/s/	See	/zh/	sure
short /a/	At	/hw/	wheel
/l/	Lip	/ng/	song
/d/	Did	/oi/	boil
/f/	Fly	/ou/	house
/h/	Him	/oo/	soon

/g/	Get	/oo/	book
short /o/	On	long /a/	aim
/k/	Kit	long /e/	ear
/m/	Man	long /i/	ice
/r/	Rat	long /o/	oat
/b/	Bin	/yoo/	use
short /e/	Elm	/th/	the
/y/	Yet	/ô/	ball
/j/	Jar	/û/	bird
short /u/	Us	/ä/	car
/w/	Wet	/a/	alarm
/v/	Vet	/â/	chair

MANTRAS OF PHONICS

Phonics instruction teaches the connection between word sounds and written letters. It's a key part of learning to read. But phonics instruction also teaches spelling patterns. For success in both reading and spelling, here are some important phonics mantras:

- *Short and long vowels*

   When a vowel is followed by one consonant, that vowel is usually short. A vowel is usually short when there is only one vowel in a word or syllable, as in on, red and fantastic.

   A vowel is long when it says its own name. When a single vowel is at the end of a word or syllable, it usually makes the long vowel sound, as in go and paper.

   Vowels also have long sounds when they're paired with a silent e or when they are vowel digraphs (two vowels paired together).

- *Vowels in syllables*

   Every syllable of every word must have at least one vowel. A vowel can stand alone in a syllable, as in unit and animal. It can also be surrounded by consonants, as in jet, shut and fantastic.

- *Silent 'e'*

   When e is the last letter in a word, and there's only one other vowel in that word, the first vowel usually says its own name and the e is silent, as in cake.

- *Consonant digraphs and blends*

  In a consonant digraph, two consonants work together to form one sound that isn't like either of the letters it's made from. Examples include chap, ship, think and photo.

  Consonant blends are groups of two or three consonants whose individual sounds can be heard as they blend together. Examples of that are clam, scrub and grasp.

- *Vowel digraphs and diphthongs*

  In a vowel digraph, when two vowels are paired together, the first one is long and the other is silent, as in boat, paint and beach.

  In a diphthong, a new speech sound is formed when two vowels are paired together, as in cloud or boil.

- *R-controlled vowels*

  When a vowel is followed by an r in the same syllable, that vowel is 'r-controlled' and is no longer short. Sometimes we refer to the r as 'bossy r' because the r 'bosses' the vowel to make a new sound, as in spark, cork, germ, birthday and burn.

- *The 'schwa' sound*

  Any vowel can make the schwa sound; it sounds like uh. Words like banana, vitamin, item and another have the schwa sound.

The schwa is only found in words with more than one syllable, but never in the 'accented' syllable. The schwa is the most common sound in the English language!

- *Soft 'c' and hard 'c' and soft 'g' and hard 'g'*

When the letter c is followed by the vowels e, i or y, it usually makes its soft sound. Examples of that are cent, circus and cytoplasm. The letter c also makes a hard sound, as in cat and cocoa.

When the letter g is followed by the vowels e, i or y, it usually makes its soft sound. Examples of that are gel, giant and gym. The letter g also makes a hard sound, as in gas, gorilla and yogurt.

- *The 'fszl' (fizzle) rule*

When f, s, z and l follow a vowel at the end of a one-syllable word, they're usually doubled, as in stuff, grass, fuzz and shell.

- *Using 'k' or 'ck'*

We use ck at the end of one-syllable word when it follows a short vowel, as in duck and trick. We use k when there's another consonant immediately following the vowel, as in task and drink.

- *The /j/ sound and the /ch/ sound*

When the /j/ sound follows a short vowel in a one-syllable word, it's usually spelled dge as in badge, hedge, bridge, dodge and smudge. (The d protects the vowel from 'magic e.')

When the /ch/ sound follows a short vowel in a one-syllable word, it's usually spelled tch as in catch, fetch, stitch, blotch and clutch. Common exceptions are the words such, much, rich and which.

- Doubling

  When adding ed or ing to a word, we double the consonant if the vowel before that consonant is short. Examples of that are gripped and winning. We don't double the consonant when the vowel is long.

- *Plural nouns*

  When a plural noun ends with s, ss, sh, ch, x or z, we add es to make it plural, as in classes, brushes and foxes. Otherwise, we just add s, as in cats.

- *Nouns ending in 'y'*

  If the common noun ends with a consonant + 'y' or 'qu' + 'y', remove the 'y' and add 'ies'. The vowels are the letters a, e, i, o and u. All other letters are consonants.

Note: Broken rules
In the English language, phonics rules are often broken. Your child will frequently come across exceptions to the rule. But your child's teacher or reading specialist will teach those, too!

PRONUNCIATION

VOWELS

Short vowels
/ɪ/ ship
/e/ pen
/æ/ man
/ʌ/ cup
/ɒ/ clock
/ʊ/ book
/ə/ a camera

Long vowels
/i:/ sheep
/a:/ heart
/ɔ:/ ball
/u:/ boot
/ɜ:/ girl

Dipthongs
eɪ/ male
/aɪ/ fine
/ɔɪ/ boy
/aʊ/ house
/əʊ/ phone
/ɪə/ year
/eə/ chair

BASIC PHONETIC CHART

Making English Sounds

single vowels

ɪ	iː	ʊ	uː
ship	sheep	book	shoot
e	ɜː	ə	ɔː
left	her	teacher	door
æ	ʌ	ɒ	ɑː
hat	up	on	far

diphthongs

eɪ	ɔɪ	aɪ
wait	coin	like
eə	ɪə	ʊə
hair	here	tourist
əʊ	aʊ	/
show	mouth	

---

unvoiced consonants

p	f	θ	t	s	ʃ	tʃ	k
pea	free	thing	tree	see	sheep	cheese	coin

voiced consonants

b	v	ð	d	z	ʒ	dʒ	g
boat	video	this	dog	zoo	television	joke	go
m	n	ŋ	h	w	l	r	j
mouse	now	thing	hope	we	love	run	you

UNIT 1 /i:/ Sheep

Target Sound: Open your mouth very little to make the target sound a long sound. Listen and repeat.

Minimal pairs

Sheep	**Leak**
Here came the sheep.	Stop it leaking.
Cheeks	**Peel**
What lovely cheeks.	This orange peel.
Bean	**Leave**
Throw out that bean.	He's going to leave.
Cheese	**Cheap**
I want some cheese.	This is a cheap shirt.
Three	**Please**
I went three pen.	Help me please.

UNIT 2 /ɪ/ Ship

- I love to eat fish. Can I eat it?
- Yes eat it.
- What about this cheese? Can I eat it?
- No, don't eat it. It's stale.

Target Sound: Open your mouth a little more to make the target sound that is short. Listen and repeat both sounds together: /i/ is long, /i;/ is short.

Minimal pairs

Sound 1	Sound 2
Look out for that sheep.	Look out for that ship.
Leak	**Lick**
Stop it leaking.	Stop it licking.
Cheeks	**Chicks**
What lovely cheeks.	What lovely chicks.
Peel	Pill
Bean	**Bin**

Little Red Book of Phonics

Throw out that bean.	Throw out that bin.
Leave	**Live**
He's going to leave.	He's going to live.

UNIT 3 /e:/ Pen

- Is this milk fresh?
- Yes. Everything in this fridge is fresh.

Target Sound: Open your mouth a little more to make the short target sound /e/. Listen and repeat both sounds together.

Minimal pairs

Sound 1	Sound 2
/i/	/e/
In needapin.	In needapen.
bin	Ben
tin	ten
It's a big tin.	It's a big ten.

pig	peg
Bill	bell
There's the bill.	There's the bell.
chick	cheque

UNIT 4 /æ/ Man

Target Sound: First practise the sound /e/. Open your mouth a little more to make the target sound. Listen and repeat. Listen and repeat both sounds together.

Minimal pairs

Sound 1	Sound 2
X	Axe
Put the axe here.	Put the axe here.
Pen	**Pan**
Can I barrow a pen?	Can I borrow a pan?
Men	**Man**
Look at the men.	Look at the man.

Send	Sand
Gem	Jam

UNIT 5 /ʌ/ Cup

- I'm hungry.
- Oh shut up. Everybody's hungry.

Target Sound: /ʌ/

First practise the sound. Listen and repeat. Put your tongue back a little to make the short target sound. Listen and repeat. Listen and repeat both sounds.

Minimal pairs

Sound 1	Sound 2
Cap	Cup
Where's my cap?	Where's my cup?

Track

There's a hat in the closet.

Ban

There's a ban on it.

Bag

She's got a bag.

Ankle

My ankle was injured.

Truck

There's a hut in the jungle.

Bun

There's a bun on it.

Bug

She's got a bug.

Uncle

My uncle was injured.

UNIT 6 /ɑ:/ Heart

- Marvellous cars, aren't they?
- Wonderful fantastic...so fast.

Target Sound: /ɑ:/

First practise the sound. Listen and repeat. Put your tongue further back and down to make the longer target sound: /a://. Listen and repeat. Listen and repeat both sounds together. In /æ/ is short, /a:/ is long.

Minimal pairs

Sound 1	Sound 2
Cap	**Carp**
What a lovely cap!	What a lovely carp!
Hat	**Heart**
He touched his hat.	He touched his heart.
Cat	**Cart**
It's a farm cat.	It's a farm cart.
Ban	**Barn**
There's a ban on it.	There's a barn on it.
Pack	**Park**
I'll pack the lunch	I'll park the car.

UNIT 7 Review

1. Beat   bit   bet   bat   but   bart

2. Bead   bid   bed   bad   bud   bard

3. Peak   pick   peck   pack   puck   park

4. Peaty   pity   petty   patty   putty   party

UNIT 8 /ɒ/ Clock

- What's wrong?
- I've got a really bad backache.
- I'm sorry to hear that.

Target Sound: /ɒ/

First practise the sound /ae/. Listen and repeat. Put your tongue slightly back and bring your lips slightly forward to make the target sound in! Listen and repeat. Listen and repeat both sounds together: /ae/ and /ɒ/.

Minimal pairs

Sound 1	Sound 2
/ae/	/ɔ/
Hat	**Hot**
It's my hat.	It's hot weather.
Cat	**Cot**
He's got a white cat.	He's got a white cot.

Fax

Look for the fax.

Sack

Put it in a sack.

Tap

Turn that tap slowly.

Backs

I can see their backs.

Fox

Look for the fox.

Sock

Put it in a sock.

Top

Turn that top slowly.

Box

I can see their box.

UNIT 9 /ɔ/ Ball

Target Sound: /ɔ:/

First practise the sound /ɒ/. Listen and repeat. The back of your tongue goes up a little more to make the long target sound: /ɔ:/. Listen and repeat. Listen and repeat both sounds together. /ɒ/ is short, /ɔ:/ is long.

Minimal pairs

Sound 1	Sound 2
Don	**Dawn**
Is your name Don?	Is your name Dawn?
Shot	**Short**
He was shot.	He was short.
Pot	**Port**
It's a small pot.	It's a small port.
Fox	**Forks**
Look for the fox.	Look for the forks.
Spot	**Sport**
I don't like these spots.	I don't like these sports.

UNIT 10 /ʊ/ Book

Target Sound: /ʊ/

First practise the sound /ɒ/. Listen and repeat. The back of your tongue goes forward and up a little more to make the target sound. Listen and repeat both of these short sounds: /ɒ/ and /ʊ/.

Minimal pairs

Sound 1	Sound 2
Pot	**Put**
Put the pot plant in the garden.	Put the plant in the garden.
Cod	**Could**
How do you spell cod?	How do you spell 'could'?
Lock	**Look**
I'll lock you up.	I'll look you up.
Rock	**Rook**
The wind blew around the rock.	The wind blew around the rook.
Box	**Books**
Give me the box.	Give me the books.

UNIT 11 /uː/ Boot

Target Sound: /uː/

First practise the sound /ʊ/. Listen and repeat. Put your tongue up and back a little more to make the long target sound /uː/. Listen and repeat. Listen and repeat both sounds together. /ʊ/ is short, /uː/ is long.

Minimal pairs

Sound 1	Sound 2
Look	Luke
Pull	**Pool**
The sign said 'Pull'.	The sign said 'Pool'.
Full	**Fool**
This isn't really full proof.	This isn't really foolproof.
Could	**Cooed**
The bird could.	The bird cooed.

UNIT 12 /ɜ:/ Girl

Target Sound: /ɜ:/

First practise the sound toil. Listen and repeat. Put your tongue forward and up a little more to make the target sound /ɜ:/. Listen and repeat. Listen and repeat both of these long sounds together: /ɔ:/ and /ɜ:/.

Minimal pairs

Sound 1	Sound 2
Four	**Fur**
She's got four.	She's got fur.
Torn	**Turn**
It's a torn sing.	It's a turn sigh.
Walker	**Worker**
He's a fast walker.	He's a fast worker.

UNIT 13 /ə/ Camera

Target Sound: /ə/

First practise the sound /ɜ:/. Listen and repeat. Make the same sound but very very short to make the target sound /ə/. Listen and repeat. Listen and repeat both sounds together: /ɜ::/ is long, /ə/ is very short.

Minimal pairs

Sound 1	Sound 2
Butt	Bat

UNIT 14 Review

/ɒ/	/ɔ:/	/ʊ/	/u:/	/ɜ:/
Foll(ow)	fall	full	pool	furl
Cod	cord	pull	fool	curd
wad	ward	could	cooed	word

UNIT 15 /eɪ/ Male

Target Sound: /eɪ/

First practise the sound /e. Then practise the short sound /i/. Listen and repeat. Join the two sounds: /eeeɪ/. Listen and repeat the target sound /eɪ/. The second part of the sound is shorter.

Minimal pairs

Sound 1	Sound 2
Pen	pain
Shed	shade
Edge	age
Wet	wait
Test	taste
Pepper	paper

UNIT 16 /aɪ/ Fine

Target Sound: /aɪ/:

First practise the long sound /ɑ:/. Then practise the short sound /ɪ/. Listen and repeat. Join the two sounds: /a:a:a:i/. Listen and repeat. The second part of the sound is shorter.

Minimal pairs

Sound 1	Sound 2
u:aɪ	
bar	buy
bark	bike
Pa	pie
Cart	kite
Heart	height

UNIT 17 /ɔɪ/ Boy

Target Sound: /ɔɪ/:

First practise the sound /ɔː/. Then practise the short sound /ɪ/. Listen and repeat. Join the two sounds: /ɔːɔːɔːɪ/. Listen and repeat the target sound /ɔɪ/. The second part of the sound is shorter.

Minimal pairs

Sound 1	Sound 2
All	**Oil**
It's all there.	It's oil there.
Ball	**Boil**
It's a ball on his head.	It's a boil on his head.
Corn	**Coin**
Look at that golden corn.	Look at that golden coin.
Tore	**Toy**
The paper tore.	The paper toy.

UNIT 18 /aʊ/ House

Target Sound: /aʊ/

First practise the sound /æ/. Then practise the sound /ʊ/. Listen and repeat. Join the two sounds: /æææʊ/. Listen and repeat the target sound /aʊ/. The second part of the sound is shorter.

Minimal pairs

Sound 1	Sound 2
Car	cow
Bar	bow
Bra	brow
Grass	grouse
Arch	ouch

UNIT 19 /əʊ/ Phone

Target Sound: /əʊ/

First practise the sound /ɜː/. Then practise the sound /ʊ/. Listen and repeat. Join the two sounds: /.ɜːɜːɜːʊ/. Listen and repeat the target sound /əʊ/. The second part of the sound is shorter.

Minimal pairs

Sound 1	Sound 2
Burn	Bone
Fern	Phone
Work	**Woke**
I work early.	I woke early.
Flirt	**Float**
He likes flirting.	He likes floating.

UNIT 20 /ɪə/ Year

Target Sound: ɪə

First practise the sound /ɪ/. Then practise the sound /ə/. Listen and repeat. Join the two sounds: ɪ ıı ə. Listen and repeat the target sound /ɪə/.

Minimal pairs

Sound 1	Sound 2
iː	ɪə
That E's too big.	That ear's too big.
Bee	**Bear**
It's a small bee.	It's a small beer.
Tea	Tear
Pea	Pier
Bead	Beard

UNIT 21 /eə/ Chair

Target Sound: /eə/

First practise /e/. Then practise /ə/. Listen and repeat. Join the two sounds: /eeeə/. Listen and repeat the target sound /eə/.

Minimal pairs

Sound 1	Sound 2
/ɪə/	/eə/
Ear	Air
Beer	Bear
Pier	Pear
Hear	Hair
Tear	Tear
Cheers!	Chairs

UNIT 22 Review

	/eɪ/	/aɪ/	/ɔɪ/	/aʊ/	/əʊ/	/ɪə/	/eə/
1	bay	buy	boy	bow (v)	bow (n)	beer	bear
2	hay	high	hoy	how	ho	here	hair
3	A	I	Oy	Ow	Oh	ear	air
4	weight	why	oy	ow	oh	ear	air

SECTION B

CONSONANTS

English sounds

voiced consonants

b	v	ð	d	z	ʒ	ʤ	g
boat	video	this	dog	zoo	television	joke	go
m	n	ŋ	h	w	l	r	j
mouse	now	thing	hope	we	love	run	you

unvoiced consonants

p	f	θ	t	s	ʃ	ʧ	k
pea	free	thing	tree	see	sheep	cheese	coin

UNIT 23 /p/ Pen

Target Sound: /p/

Listen to the sound /p/. This is an unvoiced sound.

To make the louder sound /p/ at the beginning of a word, first close your lips hard. Then push air forward in your mouth. Then quickly open your lips to release the air suddenly. Don't use your voice. Listen and repeat: /p/.

Little Red Book of Phonics

Notice that sometimes /p/ is quieter because the air isn't released suddenly.

        Up   top   help   helps   help me

Sound /p/

pin

It's a useful pin.

pen

Pen, please!

pear

Look at the yellow pear!

cap

It's an old cap.

pup

What a lively pup!

poppy

Do you like Poppy?

UNIT 24 /b/ Baby

Target Sound: /b/

Minimal pairs

Sound 1	Sound 2
/p/	/b/
Pin	**Bin**
It's a useful pin.	It's a useful bin.
pen	ben
Pear	**Bear**
Look at the yellow pear.	Look at the yellow bear.
Cap	**Cab**
It's an old cap.	It's an old cab.
Pup	**Pub**
What a lively pup!	What a lively pub!
Poppy	bobby

UNIT 25 /t/ Table

Target Sound: /t/

To make the target sound /t/ first put your tongue behind your top teeth. Then push air forward inside your mouth. Then quickly move the tip of your tongue away from your teeth to release the air suddenly. Don't use your voice. Listen and repeat /t/.

Sound /t/

Too	You too?
Sent	You sent the emails?
Cart	Is hers the red cart?
Write	Can he write well?
Train	Does this train smell?
Trunk	Is there a trunk here?

UNIT 26 /d/ Door

Target Sound: /d/

First practise the sound /d/. Listen and repeat. Use your voice to make the target sound /d/. Listen and repeat.

Listen and repeat both sounds together. /t/ is unvoiced, /d/ is voiced. Notice that sometimes /d/ is quieter because the air isn't released suddenly.

Minimal pairs

Sound 1	Sound 2
/t/	/d/
Too	**Do**
You too?	You do?
Sent	**Send**
You sent the emails?	You send the emails?
Cart	**Card**
Is the red card hers?	Is the red cart hers?
Write	**Ride**
Can he ride well?	Can he write well?
Train	**Drain**
Does this train smell?	Does this drain smell?
Trunk	drunk

UNIT 27 /k/ Key

Target Sound: /k/

To make the target sound /k/ first touch the back of the roof of your mouth with the back of your tongue. Then push air forward behind your tongue.

Sound /k/

coat

curl

class

back

UNIT 28 /g/ Girl

Target Sound /g/

First practise the sound /k/. This is an unvoiced sound. Listen and repeat. Use your voice to make the target sound /g/. Listen and repeat. Listen and repeat both sounds together. /k/ is unvoiced, /g/ is voiced. Notice that sometimes /g/ is quieter because the air isn't released suddenly. Listen.

big   bag   fig   figs   egg   eggs   example   nut   meg

Minimal pairs

Sound 1	Sound 2
/k/	/g/
Coat	Goat
Curl	Girl
class	Glass
back	Bag
Crow	Grow

UNIT 29 Review

	/p/	/b/	/t/	/d/	/k/	/g/
1	paw	bore	tore	door	core	gore
2	pill	Bill	till	dill	kill	gill

3	pay	bay	Tay	day	Kay	gay
4	p	B	tea	Dee	key	ghee'

UNIT 30 /s/ Sun

Target Sound: /s/

To make the target sound /s/ touch your top teeth with the sides of your tongue. Put the tip of your tongue forward to nearly touch the roof of your mouth. Don't use your voice.

Sue	**Bus**
That Sue was amazing.	I heard a bus.
C	**Piece**
It's pronounced /si:/.	I want the big piece.
Sip	**Price**
Sip it slowly	What's the price?

UNIT 31 /z/ Zoo

Target Sound: /z/

First practise the sound /s/. Listen and repeat. Use your voice to make the target sound /z/. Listen and repeat both sounds together: /s/ is unvoiced, /z/ is voiced.

Minimal pairs

Sound 1	Sound 2
/s/	/z/
Sue	**Zoo**
That Sue was amazing.	That Sue was amazing.
C	**Z**
Sip	Zip
It's pronounced /si:/	It's pronounced /zi:/
Bus	**Buzz**
I heard a bus.	I heard a buzz.

UNIT 32 /ʃ/ Shoe

Target Sound: First practise the sound /s/. Listen and repeat.

Then put the tip of your tongue back a little to make the unvoiced target sound /ʃ/. Listen and repeat. Listen and repeat both sounds together. Both are unvoiced: /s/ and /ʃ/.

Minimal pairs

Sound 1	Sound 2
/s/	/ʃ/
C	She
C is third.	She is third.
Sue	**Shoe**
I like Sue's.	I like shoes.
Sip	**Ship**
Sip it carefully.	Ship it carefully.
Ass	**Ash**
Look at that ass.	Look at that ash.

Sew

He won't sew it.

Puss

'Puss!' he shouted.

Show

He won't show it.

Push

'Push!' he shouted.

UNIT 33 /ʒ/ Television

Target Sound: Past practise the sound /ʃ/. Listen and repeat.

Use your voice to make the target sound /ʒ/. Listen and repeat.

Listen and repeat both sounds. /ʃ/ is unvoiced, /ʒ/ is voiced.

Sound /ʒ/

Casual

I like casual shoes.

Massage

Sportspersons like sports massage.

Occasionally

I like seeing movies occasionally.

Little Red Book of Phonics

Measure

He was measuring a shoe for a customer.

Casualty

The injured was taken to the casualty ward.

UNIT 34 /tʃ/ Chip

Target Sound: First practise the sounds /t/ and /ʃ/. Listen and repeat.

To make the target sound /tʃ/, begin to make /t/. Then slowly move your tongue from the roof of your mouth. Do it again more quickly. Don't use your voice. Listen and repeat: /tʃ/.

Minimal pairs

Sound 1	Sound 2
Ship	**Chip**
We like ships.	We like chips.
Sheep	**Cheap**
This is a sheep farm.	This is a cheap farm.

Shop

I'll buy this shop.

Cash

I couldn't cash it.

Wash

He's washing the television.

Chop

I'll buy this chop.

Catch

I couldn't catch it.

Watch

He's watching the television.

UNIT 35 /dʒ/ January

Target Sound: /dʒ/

First practise the sound /tʃ/. Listen and repeat.

Use your voice to make the target sound /dʒ/. Listen and repeat. Listen and repeat both sounds together. /tʃ/ is unvoiced, /dʒ/ is voiced.

Minimal pairs

Sound 1	Sound 2
Cheap	**Jeep**
It' a cheap type of car.	It's a jeep type of car.
Choke	**Joke**
Are you choking?	Are you joking?
Riches	**Ridges**
A land full of riches.	A land full of ridges.
H	**Age**
Do I write 'H' here?	Do I write age here?

UNIT 36 Review

/s/	/z/	/ʃ/	/ʒ/	/tʃ/	/dʒ/
1 sue	zoo	shoe	—	chew	Jew(ish)

2	Sam	(e)xam	sham	—	cham(pion) jam
3	so	zo(ne)	show	—	cho(sen) Joe
4	C	Z	she	—	chea(p) Gee!
5	sap	zap	chap(erone)	chap	Jap(anese)

UNIT 37 /f/ Fan

Target Sound: To make the target sound /f/, touch your top teeth with your bottom lip. Blow out air between your lip and your teeth. Don't use your voice. Listen and repeat: /f/.

Minimal pairs

Sound 1	Sound 2
/p/	/f/
Pin	**Fin**
It's a sharp pin.	It's a sharp fin.
Peel	**Feel**
Peel this orange.	Feel this orange.

Little Red Book of Phonics

Pull	**Full**
The sign said 'Pull'.	The sign said 'Full'.
Snip	**Sniff**
Snip these flowers.	Sniff these flowers.
Palm	**Farm**
He showed me his palm.	He showed me his farm.

UNIT 38 /v/ Van

Target Sound: First practise the sound /f/. This is an unvoiced sound. Listen and repeat. Use your voice to make the target sound /v/. Listen and repeat. Listen and repeat both sounds: /f/ and /v/.

Minimal pairs

Sound 1	Sound 2
Safe	**Save**
Safe here?	Save here?

Fine	**Vine**
Fine in the garden?	Vine in the garden?
fail	**Veil**
It's a fail.	It a veil.
Fast	**Vast**
They need a fast ship.	They need a vast ship.
Ferry	**Very**
Ferry late?	Very late?

UNIT 39 /w/ Window

Target Sound: First practise the sound /v/. Listen and repeat. Make your lips round and hard to make the short target sound /w/. Listen and repeat. Listen and repeat the two sounds: /v/ and /w/.

Minimal pairs

Sound 1

/v/

V

V didn't come before U.

Vest

That's the vest.

Vet

The dog's vet.

Vine

This is my best vine.

Veil

It's a blue veil.

Sound 2

/w/

We

We didn't come before you.

West

That's the west.

Wet

The dog's wet.

Wine

This is my best wine.

Whale

It's a blue whale.

UNIT 40 /j/ Yellow

Target Sound: First practise the sound /iː/. Listen and repeat.

To make the target sound /j/, begin to make the sound /iː/ but very quickly move your tongue to make the next sound. Do not touch the roof of your mouth with your tongue or you will make another sound like /dʒ/. Listen and repeat.

Listen and repeat both sounds: /dʒ/ and /j/.

Minimal pairs

Sound 1	Sound 2
/dʒ/	/j/
Joke	**Yolk**
That's a wonderful joke.	That's a wonderful yolk.
Juice	**Use**
There's no juice.	There's no use.

Little Red Book of Phonics

Jam	**Yam**
Would you like jam?	Would you like yam?
Jess	**Yes**
Jess I love you.	Yes, I love you.

UNIT 41 /h/ Hat

Target Sound: To make the target sound /h/, push a lot of air out very quickly. Do not touch the roof of your mouth with your tongue. Listen and repeat: /h/.

Minimal pairs

Sound 1	Sound 2
(no sound)	/h/
Ill	**Hill**
Is Terry ill?	Is Terry Hill in hospital?
And	**Hand**
Put your heart and head into it.	Put your heart, hand and head into it.

Old	**Hold**
Old Mrs Richard's hand.	Hold Mrs Richard's hand.
Ear	**Hear**
She lost her earnings.	She lost her hearing.
Islands	**Highlands**
I love the islands.	I love the highlands.

UNIT 42 /θ/ Thin

Target Sound: /θ/

To make the target sound /θ/, put your tongue between your teeth. Blow out air between your tongue and your top teeth. Do not use your voice. Listen and repeat: /θ/.

Minimal pairs

Sound 1	Sound 2
Mouse	**Mouth**
What a sweet little mouse!	What a sweet little mouth!

Little Red Book of Phonics

Sum	**Thumb**
Is this sum OK?	Is this thumb OK?
Sick	**Thick**
It's very sick.	It's very thick.
Sink	**Think**
He's sinking.	He's thinking.
Pass	**Path**
There's a mountain pass.	There's a mountain path.

UNIT 43 /ð/

Target Sound: First practise the sound /θ/. Listen and repeat. Use the voice to make the target sound /ð/. Listen and repeat both sounds: /θ/ is voiced, /ð/ is unvoiced.

Minimal pairs

Sound 1	Sound 2
Dan	**Than**
Terry is bigger, Dan.	Terry is bigger than Dan.

Day

Day arrived.

Doze

Doze after lunch.

They

They arrived.

Those

Those after lunch.

UNIT 44 Review

/z/ (zoo), /ʒ/ (television), /dʒ/ (January), /v/ (van), /w/ (windows), /j/ (yellow), /h/ (hat), /ð/ (the leather)

UNIT 45 /m/ Mouth

Target Sound: To make the target sound /m/, close your lips. Use your voice, /m/ comes through your nose. Listen and repeat: /m/.

/m/

Mile

The mile is very old.

Mine

This is mine.

Mummy

He loves his mummy.

Comb

I want a comb.

Name

He's proud of his name.

UNIT 46 /n/ Nose

Target Sound: /n/

To make the target sound /n/, don't close your lips. Put your tongue on the roof of your mouth. Touch your side teeth with the sides of your tongue. Use your voice. /n/ comes through your nose. Listen and repeat: /n/.

Minimal pairs

Sound 1	Sound 2
/m/	/n/
Mile	**Nile**
The mile is very old.	The Nile is very old.
Mine	**Nine**
This is mine.	This is nine.

Mummy	**Money**
He loves mummy.	He loves money.
Comb	**Cone**
I want a comb.	I want a cone.
Name	**Mane**
He's proud of this name.	He's proud of this mane.

UNIT 47 /ŋ/ Ring

Target Sound: To make the target sound /ŋ/, touch the back of the roof of your mouth with the back of your tongue. Use your voice. It comes through your nose. Listen and repeat: /ŋ/.

Minimal pairs

Sound 1	Sound 2
/n/	/ŋ/
Win	**Wing**
What a win!	What a wing!

Little Red Book of Phonics

Thin	**Thing**
Why this thin?	Why this thing?
Ban	**Bang**
Ban the book.	Bang the book.
Ran	**Rang**
They ran for an hour.	They rang for an hour.
Run	**Rung**
She has never run before.	She has never rung before.

UNIT 48 /l/ Letter

Target Sound: First practise the sound /n/. Listen and repeat. To make the target sound /l/, the air goes over the sides of your tongue and out of your mouth. Listen: /l/. Listen and repeat both sounds: /n/ and /l/.

Minimal pairs

Sound 1	Sound 2
/n/	/l/
No	**Low**
We need no tables.	We need low tables.
Night	**Light**
It's a bright night.	It's a bright night.
Nine	**Line**
That nine is too long.	That line is too long.
Snap	**Slap**
That's a snapping noise.	That's a slapping noise.

UNIT 49 /r/ Rain

Target Sound: To make the target sound /r/, turn the tip of your tongue up. Do not touch the roof of your mouth with your tongue. The sides of your tongue should touch your top back teeth. Listen and repeat: /r/.

Minimal pairs

Sound 1	Sound 2
/l/	/r/
Long	**Wrong**
It's a long road.	It's a wrong long road.
Load	**Road**
It's a long load.	It's long road.
Fly	**Fry**
I like to fly.	I'd like to fry it.

UNIT 50 Review

	/m/	/n/	/n/	/l/	/r/
1.	Pam	pan	pang'	pal	par(agraph)
2.	Mum	Mon(day)	mung'	mull	Murr(ay)
3.	some	sun	sung	sull(yr)	Surr(ey)
4.	Tim	tin	ring	till	tyr(anny)

INTONATION

INTONATION

Intonation is the rise and fall of the voice in speaking. This movement up or down begins on the most important word in a phrase or sentence. The pattern or melody of pitch changes in connected speech, especially the pitch pattern of a sentence, which distinguishes kinds of sentences.

Listen and repeat.

Would you like <u>coffee</u> or <u>tea</u>?

Would you like coffee, tea or milk?

Numbers

Word stress

Stressed syllables are in **bold**. Listen and repeat.

Three	thir**teen**	**thir**ty
Four	four**teen**	**for**ty
Five	fif**teen**	**fif**ty
Six	six**teen**	**six**ty
Seven	seven**teen**	**seven**ty
Eight	eigh**teen**	**eigh**ty
Nine	nine**teen**	**nine**ty

Moving stress

The stress in these 'teen' numbers is different when we are counting

thirteen, **four**teen, **fif**teen, **six**teen, **seven**teen, etc.

other moving stress

The stress in these 'teen' numbers is also different when there is a strong stress in the next word.

<u>Terry</u> lives at number fif**teen**.

<u>Terry</u> lives at number **fif**teen **Green** Street.

Intonation is the voice going up or down on the strongest syllable of the most important word in a phrase or sentence.

Intonation statement usually goes down at the end.

Intonation in the WH questions (*Who? What? Why? Where? When? How?*) usually goes down at the end.

Intonation in Yes/No questions usually goes up at the end.

Listen and repeat.

WH questions: **How** did you spend your holiday?

Statement: I **went** to Jaipur.

Yes/No question: Was it ex**pen**_____sive?

Listen and repeat.

Statement: **Yes. Very.**

No. Not very.

Stress and intonation

Stress and intonation are used to show feelings in English.

Intonation in a list

Intonation goes up on the last strongly stressed word in each phrase, and then down at the end. Listen and repeat.

He bought a **<u>cup</u>** and some **<u>nuts</u>.**

He bought a **<u>cup</u>,** some **<u>nuts</u> and some honey.**

He bought a **<u>cup</u>,** some **<u>nuts</u>** and some **<u>honey</u>** and a **<u>brush</u>.**

Intonation in exclamations

We often show the feeling of surprise in an exclamation where the intonation goes a long way up and down.

Listen and repeat.

<u>What</u> a <u>fast car</u>!

<u>What</u> a <u>mar</u>vellous <u>pho</u>tograph?

<u>What</u> a fan**tas**tic gui**<u>tar</u>**?

Intonation in suggestions and commands

Intonation is the voice going up or down. Sometimes this shows whether the speaker is more polite and friendly or less friendly.

Intonation goes up in a suggestion and this sounds polite and friendly:

<u>Have</u> a <u>holi</u>day, Mrs Brown.

<u>Stop wash</u>ing, Mr Barnes.

<u>Put</u> it on the <u>box</u>, Miss Irene.

Don't <u>drop</u> that <u>pot</u>, Ms Nikita.

Intonation goes down in a command, and this sounds less friendly:

<u>Have</u> a <u>holi</u>day, Mrs Brown.

<u>Stop wash</u>ing, Mr Barnes.

<u>Put</u> it on the <u>box</u>, Miss Irene.

Don't <u>drop</u> that <u>pot</u>, Ms Nikita.

Intonation is the voice going up or down. We can show a feeling of surprise with an intonation that goes a long way up.

Listen to the speakers expressing surprise.

A: Mr Jerry always plays football in the morning.

B: In the <u>morning?</u>

C: Mr <u>Jerry?</u>

D: <u>Football?</u>

Always?

We should put all these books in that box *now*, **should**n't we?

The intonation in most question tags is going down. This means tags are used a lot in conversations to create agreement and rapport between the speakers.

Repeat

<u>**should**</u> you? <u>**should**</u>n't you? <u>**could**</u> you? <u>**couldn't**</u> you? <u>**would**</u> he? <u>**Wouldn't**</u> he?

- He could <u>**cook**</u>, <u>**could**</u> he?
- You wouldn't <u>**look**</u>, <u>**would**</u> you?
- He could play <u>**foot**</u>ball, <u>**could**</u>n't he?
- They would like <u>**sug**</u>ar, <u>**would**</u>n't they?

Intonation: up or down tags

The intonation of question tags is usually going down. This means the speaker is not sure if the information is correct and is asking the listener to check in. Before an up tag there is often a slight pause.

- A. The nurses were at work on Thursday, weren't they?
- B. Yes, they were.

In a conversation we can show surprise by repeating the other person's words with the intonation going up.

Sentence stress

Notice how the strongly stressed words are LOUDer, and the weakly stressed words are said quickly.

A. <u>Excuse</u> me.

B. <u>Yes</u>?

A. Could you <u>tell</u> me where I can get some shoelaces?

B. Yes. There's a <u>shop</u> next to the <u>super</u>market that sells <u>very</u> good <u>shoe</u>laces. <u>I'm</u> going there <u>too</u>.

Intonation: up or down tags

The intonation of question tags is usually going down. This means the speaker expects agreement. Down tags are used a lot to create agreement and rapport between speakers.

- A: We were at work early, <u>weren't</u> we?

- B: Yes, we were.

Sometimes the intonation goes up. This means the speaker is not sure if the information is correct and is asking the listener to check in. Before an up tag there is often a slight pause.

- A: The porters were at work on Sunday, weren't they?

- B: Yes, they were.

Unstressed words and syllables

The spelling has been changed in the words on the right to show you when to use the sound /ə/.

photograph of	ə photəgraph əf
a glass of water	ə glass of wat ə
a pair of binoculars	ə pair əf binoculəs
photograph of her father and mother	photəgraph əf hə fathə and mothər
a book about South America	ə book əbout South əmericə]

In a conversation we can show surprise by repeating the other person's words with the intonation going up.

A: I'm afraid you've made a mistake, sir.   B: A mis<u>take</u>.

A: They changed the timetable.   B: <u>Changed</u> it?

Stress in phrasal verbs

1. He's sitting <u>down</u>.
2. He's lying <u>down</u>.
3. He's <u>standing</u> up.
4. He's <u>turning</u> round.

Little Red Book of Phonics

5. He's <u>shout</u>ing out.

6. He's <u>runn</u>ing around.

The letter 'r'—pronounced or silent?

When there is no vowel following it, /r/ is silent. This 'rule' only applies to some speakers of English. But many speakers always pronounce /r/.

'r' not pronounced	'r' pronounced (before a vowel)
Here they are.	Here- are- all the books
Here's the beer.	The beer- is here- on the table.

Stress and intonation

A <u>pin</u>	a <u>pen</u>cil	a paper <u>plate</u>
A pen	a postcard	a pepper pot
A pear	a picture	a plastic spider
Some soap	a carpet	a piano

Intonation usually goes down on the last strongly stressed word in a sentence. In a list, the intonation goes up with each item but down on the last item.

He bought a <u>pen</u>.

He bought a <u>pen</u> and <u>pen</u>cil.

He bought a <u>pen</u> and <u>pen</u>cil and a pin.

In compound nouns, the stress is on the first word.

1. a **shelf**   a **book**shelf
2. a **brush**   a **hair**brush   a **paint**brush
3. a **card**   a **post**card   a **birth**day card
4. a **ball**   a **foot**ball   a **ping** pong ball
5. a **bag**   a **hand**bag   a **shopp**ing bag
6. a **man**   a po**lice**man   a **post**man

Intonation in questions: new information/old information

In yes/no questions, intonation usually begins to go up on the most important word for the speaker's meaning.

- Could you tell me the <u>time</u>, please?

In WH questions, intonation usually begins to go down on the most important word for the speaker's meaning.

- What's the <u>time</u> please?
- How do I get to the <u>sports</u> avenue?
- <u>Where's</u> the <u>toilet</u>, please?

Notice that intonation in *WH* questions can change when we are talking about old information. The first time we ask somebody's name, we ask: <u>*What's*</u> *your* <u>*name*</u>? *This is new information*. If we forget the name and ask again: <u>*What's your*</u> <u>*name*</u>? because we are asking about old information that has already been given. Intonation goes up to show that this is something we have already shared.

Little Red Book of Phonics

Sentence stress patterns

(adjective + noun)

1. A <u>clean</u> <u>shelf</u>.   A clean <u>book</u>shelf.
2. A <u>white</u> <u>cup</u>.   A white <u>coffee</u> cup.
3. A <u>plastic</u> <u>ring</u>.   A plastic <u>key</u> ring.
4. A <u>dirty</u> <u>bottle</u>.   A dirty <u>cola</u> bottle.
5. An <u>electric</u> <u>clock</u>.   An electric <u>cuckoo</u> clock.
6. An <u>expensive</u> <u>cake</u>.   An expensive <u>chocolate</u> cake.

Intonation in thanks/responses

We usually say thank you and reply to thank you with intonation going down at the end. When somebody says 'Thank you' for doing something, we sometimes reply, 'It's a pleasure', or 'My pleasure'. Some other responses are: 'You're welcome', 'That's all right', 'That's OK'.

Stress and intonation: highlighting a word

1. <u>Did</u> you live in New Delhi?

Suggests the meaning: (There are different opinions about this. What's the truth.)

2. Did <u>you</u> used to live in New Delhi?

Suggests: (I did. Or somebody else did. What about you?)

3. Did you <u>use</u> to live in New Delhi?

Suggests: (But not now.)

4. Did you used to <u>live</u> in New Delhi?

Suggests: (But maybe you worked somewhere else)

5. Did you used to live in <u>New Delhi</u>?

Suggests: (But not some other city)

A sentence can have five different meaning as given below by a change in intonation:

1. <u>He</u> had a red car. (But not anymore. Now now.)

2. He <u>had</u> a red car. (But nobody else did.)

3. He had <u>a</u> red car. (Not a car or any kind of vehicle.)

4. He had a <u>red</u> car. (Just one. Not several of them.)

5. He had a red <u>car</u>. (Not a yellow one or any other colour.)

Intonation

Exclamation

Oh <u>dear</u>?

How <u>horri</u>ble!

How <u>aw</u>ful!

How <u>terri</u>ble!

Word linking with /h/

In rapid spoken English, words are sometimes linked by the disappearance of the sound /h/

1. Who found him?
2. What's his name? Harry?
3. Who else have you spoken to? She's his wife?
4. What has the neighbour said about him?
5. What had she eaten?

'Mm' has many meanings, depending on the intonation.

- Mmm means 'What did you say?'
- Mm means 'yes'
- Mmmmm means 'How nice!'
- Mmm…means 'I'm thinking about what you say.

Remember if one speaks without intonation the meaning that one desire to express falls flat. Reaffirm what you want to express.